First published in February 1999 by the Audit Commission for Local Authorities and the National Health Service in England and Wales, 1 Vincent Square, London SW1P 2PN.

Printed in the UK for the Audit Commission by Kent Litho.

ISBN 1 86240 146 2

Illustrations by Patrick MacAllister.

# Introduction

## Why has this paper been written?

**1.** Over the last ten years, councils, police forces and fire brigades have recognised the need to set standards and targets for their services. Such targets and standards have helped them to make it clear to staff what levels of performance they should achieve, and to the public what levels of performance they can expect. Initially, the kinds of standards adopted by local authorities tended to be general statements of good will: promises to be polite and courteous, to put lids back on dustbins, or to keep streets clean. But as more authorities developed performance review systems, some began to adopt standards that were more rigorous and committed the organisation to measurable levels of achievement. And the best incorporated these into performance review systems: setting targets, measuring achievement, reporting performance and reviewing targets to achieve continuous improvement.

**2.** In practice, however, few local authorities have gone this far. Even though some pioneers were introducing comprehensive performance review systems almost ten years ago, the use of service standards and targets is still patchy, with many local authorities setting targets or service standards but not monitoring achievement. And service standards that are fully integrated into performance review systems are rarer still. But this is not just a problem for local government: other public sector organisations and private sector companies have also often found it difficult to get their performance monitoring arrangements right.

*Under best value, setting targets and service standards, and measuring their achievement, will be even more important.*

**3.** Under best value, setting targets and service standards, and measuring their achievement, will be even more important. The Government's recent White Papers (Refs. 1 and 2) make this clear:

'locally set targets in respect of strategic objectives, efficiency, effectiveness, quality and fair access in respect of all key services should be underpinned by a minimum requirement for improvement ... the framework of targets will put most pressure on those authorities who are currently performing poorly on both the quality and efficiency with which they deliver services.'

*Most authorities have a long way to go if they are to set up the kind of arrangements that will be needed by April 2000, when best value is likely to become a statutory responsibility.*

**4.** So not only will authorities be required to set a wide range of targets for their services, they will also have to measure achievement and demonstrate that improvements are being made, especially where services have performed poorly in the past. Authorities will also need to consult local people on local standards and report past performance in local performance plans.

**5.** Most authorities have a long way to go if they are to set up the kind of arrangements that will be needed by April 2000, when best value is likely to become a statutory responsibility. They should start now to establish performance monitoring systems and to think about how they can set and monitor targets. If they do not, they will find it difficult to satisfy local people, the Government, auditors and other commentators that they have achieved best value.

**6.** This management paper looks at how councils, police forces and fire brigades currently use service standards and targets and gives guidance on how to set standards and targets, and how to measure their achievement. It also looks at how local communities can be involved in this process, and how local authorities can improve their accountability to the public by using standards and targets. It looks at:

- why local standards and targets matter;
- what authorities are doing now;
- how to set targets;
- how to measure achievement;
- how to involve staff, authority members and the public; and
- future developments.

## Who has this paper been written for?

**7.** This paper has been written to help local authorities to respond to the proposed new duty to secure best value. It is particularly aimed at councillors, members of police and fire authorities and officers in councils, police and fire authorities who are involved in setting, monitoring and achieving local performance standards. It may also be of interest to consumer and community organisations, government departments and all those with an interest in local authority performance.

## The evidence on which this paper is based

**8.** This paper is based on a national survey of local authorities, and on specific case studies of good practice. The efforts made by the best organisations show that any local authority could, and should, begin to set up the structures that are necessary to use local standards and targets effectively. The authorities cited as case studies in this paper are not, of course, the only ones that are already making good use of local performance indicators.

## Terminology

**9.** Throughout this paper, local targets and standards[I] are defined as follows:

***Standards*** are promises that are made to service users about the levels and quality of service that they can expect. For example 'We promise to collect domestic refuse on the stated day each week, replace the lid on your bin, close your gate, and leave the area clean and tidy.'

***Targets*** are commitments that are made in advance to achieve a stated level of service. For example 'Percentage of benefit applications processed in 14 days: 95 per cent.'

***Performance measures*** are systems to collect data that demonstrate how well a standard is being achieved or whether a target is being met. For example 'Percentage of missed bins which were put right within 24 hours during 1997/98 = 85 per cent.'

---

I This paper is concerned with locally defined and set targets and standards. The term 'standard' is used here with a slightly different meaning from that specified in a national context in Section 4 of the Local Government Bill.

# 1. Why local standards and targets are important

**10.** There are eight reasons why setting local standards and targets is important. Properly monitored targets and standards:

- focus attention on exactly what kind of service is needed, making it clear to staff, authority members and the public what level of service is expected;
- help front-line managers to focus effort and resources on priorities;
- help authorities to know when to adjust services and resources according to the authority's policy priorities;
- provide a route for involving the public in planning future services;
- help organisations to develop a culture of continuous improvement;
- put national performance standards into a local context;
- help authority members to hold staff and contractors to account for performance; and
- help the public and service users to see whether services are being delivered efficiently and effectively and to hold authority members to account for performance.

**11.** Performance targets have been used in central government to monitor the work of the Next Steps agencies from soon after the first of these agencies was set up in 1988. There are now well over 100 agencies, each with a set of service and financial performance targets. More recently, a performance-based approach has been introduced to central government departments as part of the Government's comprehensive spending review [CASE STUDY 1].

**12.** Local and national governments in other countries are also now using published targets and standards as a way of making government more accountable and efficient. Over the last six years, the United States federal government, the world's largest employer, has undergone a cultural and structural change called 'Reinventing Government' [CASE STUDY 2, overleaf]. At the heart of this change has been a requirement for government departments and agencies to set up comprehensive performance review systems, standards and targets. The scale of this exercise, and the savings that it has apparently achieved, demonstrate the value of proper targeting and monitoring, particularly where this is centrally driven and co-ordinated.

**13.** In Britain, large public sector organisations outside of government have used published standards as a way of making themselves more accountable to the public. Each year the BBC publishes a *Statement of Promises*, showing its performance against a set of specific indicators along with targets for the coming year. This initiative has helped the BBC to demonstrate that it is shaping its service to meet the needs of licence payers, and to focus on those areas that consumer research has shown to be of greatest public concern [CASE STUDY 3, overleaf].

*Large public sector organisations have used published standards as a way of making themselves more accountable to the public.*

CASE STUDY 1

**Performance targets in central government departments**

Performance targets are now being applied systematically to central government departments in a process set out in *Modern Public Services* (Ref. 3) in July 1998. This paper announced the results of the comprehensive spending review and set out departmental goals to be achieved by the end of the Parliament. It also announced the intention to introduce 'public service agreements' between each department and the Treasury, setting out measurable efficiency and effectiveness targets against which progress will be monitored. The agreements were published in a Cabinet Office White Paper in December 1998 (Ref. 4).

The core principles underpinning the public service agreements are:

- better co-ordination across different parts of government;
- improving efficiency and strengthening incentives to improve performance by linking achievement of targets to spending plans;
- more responsiveness to users; and
- greater openness by making available more information on the quality and efficiency of departments' work.

Most of the targets that have been agreed are clear and measurable. For example, the Lord Chancellor's Department's targets include:

- reducing the waiting time for all asylum appeals from receipt ... to determination from 36 weeks in 1999/2000 to 17 weeks by 31 March 2002;
- halving the time from arrest to sentence for persistent young offenders from 142 days to 71 days by 31 March 2002; and
- increasing the proportion of mediated as against court-based divorce proceedings from 5 to 20 per cent by 2001/02 for those areas where the Family Law Act is implemented.

The targets that have been agreed are clearly related to each department's objectives and each has a timescale. In some areas, not all objectives have precise targets yet, so further measures are being developed. In the interim, intermediate milestones have been identified to help to gauge progress towards objectives.

*Source: Cabinet Office briefing note*

CASE STUDY 2

**National Partnership for Reinventing Government (NPRG): using targets on a big scale**

In 1993, President Clinton instigated a national performance review of the United States civil service. The purpose of this review was to make 150 government agencies more performance-based. Performance review systems were introduced that focused on the expectations of customers and the organisations' outcomes. The agencies were required to establish 'customer service standards' – 1,500 such standards were created in the first year. These reviews led to government legislation to abolish obsolete regulations and to create new partnerships between government agencies and their users. Benchmarking between agencies was also introduced, to make sure that benefits from the changes were shared across all government departments.

Several key principles were used as the basis of the reinvention process, including:

- improving customer services by setting measurable targets;
- increasing partnership working;
- establishing single contact points for people needing to deal with federal government; and
- extensive training, as part of a cultural change intended to encourage government employees to embrace all these principles in the way that they approached their work.

Central to this process was the setting of performance indicators for each agency to make sure that the achievement of targets could be measured. In recent years, the NPRG has concentrated on applying the good practice, which has emerged in some agencies, across government as a whole. These 'rules of reinvention' have been communicated to everyone responsible for running government agencies through a good practice checklist.

To date, the NPRG's main claimed achievements have been:

- achieving over $137 billion dollars in savings;[1]
- sponsoring 850 'labour-managed' organisations, where the workforce are actively involved in the reinvention process;
- introducing 4,000 customer standards in 570 organisations; and
- achieving the first increase in public trust in federal government (through opinion polls) for 30 years – although the NPRG admits that this may not be entirely due to the reinvention process!

1 Details of these savings can be found on http://www.npr.gov/library/papers/bkgrd/explain.html

*Source: NPRG website: http://www.npr.gov*

CASE STUDY 3

**The BBC: using targets for public accountability**

In 1996, the BBC's new charter stated that the corporation should 'publish and make available an annual statement of promises'. This statement was to include the BBC's key targets for each coming year, against which it would report its performance.

The first of these statements of promises was published in 1996. To decide what the promises should be, the BBC used extensive market research, and consulted national consumer groups, voluntary sector bodies and special interest groups, including those representing, for example, people with disabilities and ethnic minority communities. After analysing this feedback, the governors adopted a comprehensive statement, with over 230 promises. However, this was found to be too many and made it difficult to focus on those issues that were of most concern to the public.

So, for the following year, the number of promises was reduced, concentrating on issues that were of most concern to viewers and listeners, that were clearly measurable, and that represented areas where the BBC wanted to demonstrate continuous improvement. The current year's statement of promises is published with figures showing the BBC's performance against its promises in the previous year. These results, and market research showing the public's reaction to them, are used by the governors in reviewing the BBC's core aims and objectives.

In the 1998 *Statement of Promises*, the achievement of the previous promises is shown. These include:

- *providing more factual programming during peak time on television than other broadcasters.* Fifty-one per cent of BBC 1's peak-time programming was factual (compared with 31.9 per cent on ITV and 35.6 per cent on Channel 5). On BBC 2, the figure was 50.4 per cent (compared with 50.2 per cent on Channel 4); and
- *reducing licence evasion and collection costs from their current level of 13.1 per cent of the licence fee.* Costs came down to 12.6 per cent for 1997/98.

The *Statement of Promises* also makes it clear where targets were not achieved:

- *ensure that at least eight in every ten hours of programming in television is made in the UK.* There was an improvement, but the BBC fell short of this target for the second year running. In 1997/98, 78 per cent of BBC programmes were made in the UK (compared with 77 per cent last year).

The *Statement of Promises* and figures for past performance are published in the BBC's annual report, and on the BBC's website.

*Source: BBC website http://www.bbc.co.uk, and Audit Commission research*

**14.** In the private sector too, some companies have used performance indicators and targets extensively to ensure that their corporate objectives are met, and to make themselves accountable to their customers. The Body Shop approach is an interesting example of this **[CASE STUDY 4]**.

**15.** Some local authorities have also found that published targets have helped them to make the best use of resources, and to focus efforts on those areas that are of most concern to the public. Councillors have told us that setting measurable targets, and then receiving reports on whether those targets have been met, gives them a grip on the organisation's reins that they would not otherwise have. By contrast, members of authorities with no published standards or local performance indicators can feel out of touch **[BOX A]**.

*Some local authorities have also found that published targets have helped them to make the best use of resources, and to focus efforts on those areas that are of most concern to the public.*

**BOX A**

'We have been running a comprehensive performance review system for more than six years now, with a wide range of targets, all of which are set and monitored by members at committees. Now the system has become so well-established, it is difficult for most members to imagine how they could function without it. It gives us a very easy way of seeing how well the council is running, whether it's getting better or worse, and whether we're meeting our agreed priorities.'

- *Councillor in a Midlands district council*

'We have no local performance indicators or targets to speak of, and no performance review system. That means we're reliant purely on the rather limited Audit Commission indicators or the advice of officers about whether a service is doing well or badly. Usually we hear about the real failures when members of the public tell us about them. Otherwise it makes it very difficult to get a grip on what's really going on.'

- *Councillor in a south east district council*

CASE STUDY 4

### The Body Shop: ethical auditing

The Body Shop publishes a biannual Values Report showing how the company has performed in what it terms its ethical auditing indicators and targets. Ethical auditing covers three principal areas:

- human rights (including staff rights and development, trading with communities in need, and health and safety policies);
- environmental sustainability (including purchasing policies, working with local communities and procedures for working with environmentally sensitive sites); and
- animal protection (including campaigning against animal testing and promoting animal welfare policies).

The company has established over 150 indicators and targets covering these areas, all of which are measurable. Ethical auditing focuses on areas that are identified initially through consultation with staff, customers, suppliers, and franchisees. Results of stakeholder feedback inform the target-setting process. Targets are a mixture of one-off targets (to be achieved by a particular date) and percentage achievement targets. These include:

- increasing the amount of refills of refillable products to 5 per cent;
- ensuring that 60 per cent of customers do not take a plastic carrier bag;
- ensuring that all the wood used in shops is from sustainable sources by the year 2000; and
- reducing average energy use per shop to 35,000 KWh per annum.

In some cases, complex scoring systems are used to develop simple targets. For example, the company has developed a 'star' system to assess the environmental impact of suppliers' operations. This has allowed the development of a target to double the number of suppliers with a three-star rating by the year 2000.

The levels at which targets are set are designed to challenge the organisation, but consultation is used to make sure that staff are also committed to achieving them. Targets are kept 'alive' through an ongoing monitoring process and communication with staff on interim achievement of targets, including publication of internal league tables.

Results are externally verified, and fed back to stakeholders' groups for their comments. These comments are then used to set new targets, and to review policies, in a cyclical process that is designed to achieve continuous improvement. Agreed targets are factored into the company's annual budget-setting process.

*Source: Audit Commission research*

**16.** Although all local authorities have to report their performance against the Audit Commission indicators each year, more detailed indicators are needed to fully represent council, police and fire performance locally. The Audit Commission indicators apply national standards and provide useful comparative data, because they are collected in the same way by all local authorities. But they do not address local issues and therefore cannot tell members and officers how well their authority is performing against locally agreed objectives and priorities, or provide the detail that front-line managers need to monitor the day-to-day functioning of their services.

**17.** But the principal reasons why councils, police forces and fire brigades should set targets are to help them to improve the efficiency and effectiveness of their services [BOX B] and to support accountability to local people.

BOX B

### Using targets to improve performance

#### West Mercia police force

The force target for answering letters in 1997/98 was 75 per cent in ten days. When 80 per cent were answered within ten days in 1997/98, the target was increased to 80 per cent for 1998/99.

In 1996/97, 73 crimes per thousand people were recorded in the force area. The force set a target for 1997/98 of 72. Actual performance for the year was 66, so the target for 1998/99 has now been revised to 65.

#### South Somerset District Council

A target for paying housing benefit in 14 days was set at 95 per cent in 1994/95, when actual performance was 74 per cent. Performance has improved year-on-year to 96 per cent in 1996/97, and the target has now been revised to 97.5 per cent.

#### Redditch Borough Council

This council has used targets linked to local performance indicators to target areas of specific local importance. In 1994/95, the council set a target of removing 90 per cent of abandoned vehicles in 24 hours, and achieved an actual performance of 96 per cent. In the following year, the target was raised to 95 per cent, and 98 per cent performance was achieved.

In all three authorities, officers believe that setting targets has helped to improve performance because it has helped to focus attention on these services and bring about improvements that may not otherwise have been made. For example, in West Mercia, new crime prevention initiatives were introduced because the force had publicly committed itself to a target to reduce crime. And in all three authorities, services for which targets have been set have shown more significant improvements than those services that were not subject to targets.

**18.** Although local performance standards and targets are important in themselves, and will be a vital part of best value, even the best performance indicators cannot tell you everything you might want to know about how a service is performing. The Commission has often said in the past that performance indicators should be treated as can-openers; that is, as a starting point for exploring performance fully. Indicators need to be interpreted carefully and on their own are rarely sufficient to make definitive judgements. Some important aspects of services cannot easily be measured through performance indicators, so other sorts of information - such as detailed feedback from service users and reviews by external inspectorates - are needed to provide a complete picture.

**19.** As authorities develop comprehensive systems of local indicators, they will need to avoid some pitfalls. One of the most common is that targets can distort behaviour: if staff are encouraged to focus on one aspect of performance that is being measured, other parts of the service can be adversely affected. For example, empty council homes may be relet more quickly if prospective tenants are restricted to one offer only. An excessive focus on particular targets can also be self-defeating if it results in performance data being manipulated. Improved performance and better accountability are not likely to be achieved unless authorities avoid these sorts of pitfalls. One helpful step is to make sure that systems of indicators are properly balanced; that is, that they do not concentrate on narrow aspects of performance. Authorities also need to collect data in ways that prevent performance being misreported. The rest of this paper aims to help authorities to ensure that their local systems of indicators and targets are well-designed and purposeful.

*Even the best performance indicators cannot tell you everything you might want to know about how a service is performing.*

# 2. How authorities use targets and standards now

**20.** Although best value will require councils, police forces and fire brigades to set a wide range of local performance standards and targets, relatively few authorities have comprehensive systems now. The way that authorities use targets and standards varies greatly, with some having a much more sophisticated approach than others. Overall, our survey shows that:

- more than 80 per cent of authorities do not have a comprehensive set of local targets,[1] using them only for a limited range of services;
- many authorities that do have targets do not monitor whether they are achieved. For complaints and housing, for example, around three-quarters of councils have standards, but only half measure whether they achieve them;
- unitary, metropolitan and London authorities are much more likely to set standards and targets than district and county councils. For example, more than two-thirds of London boroughs have targets for educational attainment, but only one-third of county councils have them;
- over three-quarters of authorities make information on standards and targets available to the public, most commonly through leaflets at offices. Only one-quarter distribute this sort of information directly to households;
- nine out of ten unitary and metropolitan councils report regularly to councillors on performance, but only six out of ten counties do so; and
- overall, only four out of ten authorities consult the public before they set standards and targets. Again, some types of authorities are more likely to do this than others: while three-quarters of unitaries consult the public in some way, only one-quarter of district councils do so.

*It is worrying that some authorities do not make information on their targets and whether they achieve them available to the public.*

1 That is, local standards and targets covering at least 75 per cent of the service areas covered by our survey.

**21.** Many authorities have a long way to go if they are to meet the expected requirements of best value, especially in terms of public consultation on standards and performance. It is worrying that some authorities do not make information on their targets and whether they achieve them available to the public or, in some cases, even to authority members. And while it is encouraging that most authorities do set targets for at least some services, a significant proportion do not monitor their performance against them, and so they do not know whether they are achieving them or not. There is little point in setting targets without also setting up effective monitoring systems to find out whether they are being met. Councils, police forces and fire brigades that do not monitor whether they achieve their targets should address this now – unmonitored targets will not be good enough to demonstrate that best value is being achieved.

# 3. How to set targets and standards

**22.** This section looks at how councils, police forces and fire brigades should set targets and what factors they should take into consideration. It discusses:

- what makes a good target?
- what kinds of target can be set?
- what timescales should be set for achieving targets?
- which aspects of a service should have targets?
- at what levels should targets be set?
- how many targets should be set?
- how can quality be measured?
- how can organisations set inter-agency targets?

## What makes a good target?

**23.** A good target should:

- relate to a service or corporate objective;
- be achievable but also stretch the organisation;
- have a clear, stable definition so that achievement can be compared over time;
- be easily understood;
- have the commitment of authority members and staff;
- be readily measurable;
- have a named officer responsible for its achievement; and
- be honest and unambiguous (that is, it should mean what it appears to mean).

Some of these issues are dealt with in more detail in later sections on involving staff, authority members, and the public in setting targets. Many of the characteristics of a good target concern the way that it is set and reported, rather than how it is expressed, but the kinds of targets used, and their value, vary [BOX C] .

**BOX C**

### Some targets used by councils

The following targets are clear, can be easily monitored, and help councillors to see whether objectives are being achieved:

- We will admit all children without a school place to primary schools within 15 days.
  – *London Borough of Newham*
- We will cut the proportion of waste going to landfill sites from 90 per cent to less than 50 per cent by 2005.
  – *Kent County Council*
- We will aim to achieve 100 per cent satisfaction with the range of materials available in libraries (based on a survey of library users).
  – *North Lincolnshire Council*

But these are not so useful:

- We will buy as many library books as possible.
  – *a county council*
- We will ensure value for money by providing financial support for bus services.
  – *a unitary council*
- We will improve customer complaints or explain increases.
  – *a district council*

**24.** The commonest pitfalls in devising targets and standards are either to make them easy to measure and hard to understand, or easy to understand but hard to measure **[BOX D]**. In some cases however, apparently 'unmeasurable' targets can be assessed by consumer surveys (this was done in the second example in Box D).

## What kinds of target can be set?

**25.** There are several kinds of targets. The type to choose will depend on the purpose and audience of the target. The main sorts of targets are 'all-the-time' targets, percentage achievement targets, qualitative targets, time-bound targets, national targets, and regional or family targets.

### 'All-the-time' targets

**26.** These are often called 'promises' – for example, 'we will send you an accurate council tax bill each year at least two weeks before any payments are due' (York City Council). They are useful to help the public to understand what level of service they can expect to receive 'all the time'. But they are not very versatile tools, and make it difficult to adjust services according to changing priorities. An authority may, for example, want to reduce its target for answering letters from a 'promise' to answer 100 per cent in seven days to a 'percentage achievement' target of 90 per cent in seven days. But if it revised its promise to 100 per cent in six days, it would be difficult for members and officers to know whether performance against the new standard was better or worse than against the old one.

**BOX D**

**Published standards for refuse collection**

'99.86 per cent, based on the permitted defect rate of 720 points per four-week period (as specified in the CCT refuse collection contract) divided by the number of bins emptied in a year.'
- *A metropolitan council*

'We will collect your refuse once a week, taking care to replace your bin, put the lid back on, clear up any spillage and close your gate. If we do not collect from you - for example, if the gate is locked, we will put a note through your door giving the reason why and we will pick up the following week as usual.'
- *A district council*

## Percentage achievement targets

**27.** These are commitments to achieve a stated level of performance against a standard (for example, the Department of Environment, Transport and the Regions (DETR) has set a national standard for councils to process 80 per cent of all planning applications within eight weeks). Around one-quarter of police forces and one-third of councils set this kind of target for answering telephones. But these targets are not as helpful to members of the public as 'all-the-time' targets because they do not make it clear what level of service they can expect. Promises to answer '90 per cent of calls within three rings' could be misleading – if you have to wait 20 rings, were you just part of the unlucky 10 per cent? As a tool for public accountability, percentage targets can be counter-productive, generating public cynicism because people cannot know from their own experience whether the 'promise' was being kept or not. But they are useful for authority members and service managers to adjust services or improve targets year-on-year to demonstrate continuing improvement. And a few authorities have found this type of target useful in more sophisticated public consultation. The London Borough of Lewisham, for example, has used its 'citizen's panel' to determine which services should be subject to service standards and targets, and is now using focus groups drawn from the citizen's panel to help them to decide the levels at which these targets should be set.

*As a tool for public accountability, percentage targets can be counter-productive, generating public cynicism because people cannot know from their own experience whether the 'promise' was being kept or not.*

## Qualitative targets

**28.** These targets make descriptive promises about the kind of service that people can expect – for example, 'youth work premises will be appealing, attractive, safe and maintained in such a way as to encourage the presence of young people' (Cornwall County Council). They can be easier to understand than lists of indicators and percentages, which local people may find difficult to make sense of. But they can also be open to different interpretation unless they are very precisely worded. The example in Box D includes a promise to leave the area around householders' rubbish bins 'clean and tidy'. But what if the area where the bin was placed was a mess before the refuse collectors arrived? Achievement of the stated standard may be difficult to measure without consumer satisfaction surveys. Nevertheless, this kind of target can be useful if carefully worded, especially for services where precise numerical targets do not really tell people what kind of service is on offer.

## Time-bound targets

**29.** These make a specific one-off promise – for example, 'we will work with parish councils to place 100 mini-recycling banks in outlying villages by the end of the year' (South Somerset Council). Time-bound targets are often of significant public interest, but it is important that they are tied to specified target dates – to state that achievement of a target is 'ongoing' is not helpful.

**30.** Time-bound targets are particularly useful in activities that operate over long time cycles, such as drawing up local structural plans. But they do not usually provide any comparative information. They can, however, be combined with other relevant time-bound targets to give a 'reusable' target. For example: 'We will complete 95 per cent of capital schemes within published target dates'.

## National targets

**31.** This is not so much a type of target as a source from which local targets can be derived. The Audit Commission incorporates several national targets prescribed by government or Parliament within its performance indicators – for example, the processing of benefit claims within 14 days or the determination of planning applications within 8 weeks. These national targets are useful locally because they provide comparative information. Under best value, the Government will require councils to set targets in some areas, such as educational attainment, that will relate to new national targets.

## Regional or family targets

**32.** Some councils, police forces and fire brigades have established groups of neighbouring or similar authorities to develop indicators and targets that are both locally relevant and provide comparative data. Working together in this way, authorities can also look at those that are performing to higher standards at lower costs, and share good practice ideas. However, authorities setting up groups like this should be aware of the work that is required to get useful data. Nevertheless, the results in terms of useful comparative data and shared ideas to make services run more efficiently can be invaluable [**BOX E**].

**BOX E**

**Benchmarking clubs**

'When some officers in Wycombe got involved in benchmarking clubs, they found it took up much more time than they had expected. And then the results from shared performance indicators didn't work because people were not measuring things the same way and we ended up comparing apples with pears rather than apples with apples. I think benchmarking clubs can be very useful, but everyone in the club needs to be to be fully committed to get decent results out of it.'

*– Head of Strategic Development, Wycombe District Council*

## What timescales should be set for achieving targets?

**33.** Targets are normally applied to a specified monitoring period. However, councils, police forces and fire brigades should also set targets for longer periods, where the aim is to achieve continuous improvement over a longer timescale. They may set 'secondary' targets to achieve this. For example: 'We will process 80 per cent of our housing benefit applications within 14 days by April 1998, and 90 per cent by September 1998.'

**34.** Setting targets in this way can help the authority to plan out the programme of improvement that it intends to achieve, and can provide a clear message to staff and the public that performance improvement is a continuous process, rather than just the achievement of short-term targets.

**35.** Under best value, the Government has proposed that councils, police forces and fire brigades will be required to set targets against some national indicators that will bring local performance up to the standard of the top 25 per cent of authorities. Authorities will have five years to achieve this in each service area, but their annual stepping-stone targets will need to be demonstrably consistent with the five-year target. Achieving this will be a major challenge for the majority of authorities, especially those that are currently performing relatively poorly. Analysis of performance over the last four years shows that, in services such as reletting council homes, only 1 per cent of the poorest performing councils and 4 per cent of the group above them managed this level of improvement.

*Under best value, the Government has proposed that councils, police forces and fire brigades will be required to set targets against some national indicators that will bring local performance up to the standard of the top 25 per cent of authorities.*

## Which aspects of a service should have targets?

**36.** Most local authority services can be seen in terms of inputs, outputs and outcomes. 'Inputs' are what goes into a service – money, staff resources, buildings, etc. 'Outputs' are what the service produces. And 'outcomes' are what happens as the result of a service. The relationship between these principles can be summarised using council tax collection as an example **[EXHIBIT 1]**. To get a complete picture of how a service is performing, authorities need to develop indicators to measure inputs, outputs and outcomes. Inputs may be subject to targets as a way of controlling the costs of a service, but authorities are more likely to concentrate on developing targets for outputs and outcomes.

**37.** For most services, it is easier to set output targets than outcome targets. For example, an output target for the benefits service may be the percentage of benefit claims processed in 14 days. But what should the outcome target be? What is supposed to happen as a result of the benefits service? One target could be that 100 per cent of those entitled to benefits actually claim them. But how can this be measured?

**38.** In many cases, the desired outcome of a service may be aspirational or take a long time to achieve. It may also not be entirely under the authority's control – for example, reducing the number of crimes through crime prevention work, or reducing the number of food poisoning cases through food premises inspections. Although the authority may not be wholly accountable for an outcome, that does not mean that it cannot be the subject of a target – if the council, police force or fire brigade seeks to influence an outcome (and spends money doing so), then it ought to be able to demonstrate an effect on that outcome.

EXHIBIT 1

### The relationship of inputs, outputs and outcomes

Most services can be seen in terms of inputs, outputs and outcomes. This example shows some inputs, outputs and outcomes of council tax collection.

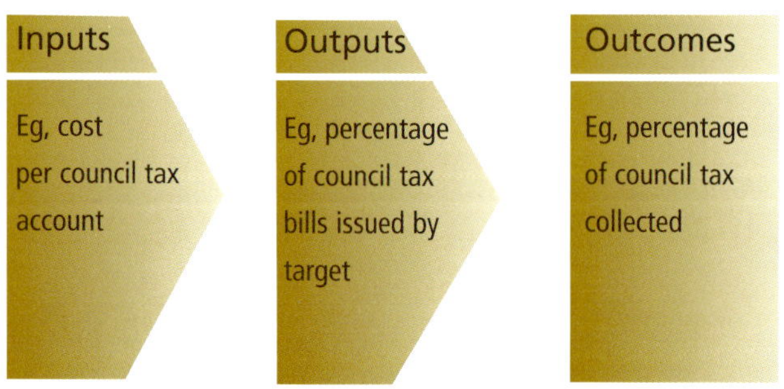


*Source: Audit Commission*

**39.** Outcomes of a service should be considered in terms of the 'ripple effect', where the service itself is seen as a stone tossed into a pond **[EXHIBIT 2]**. The immediate effects of the service, the inner ripples, are relatively easy to measure because they are closely connected to the service and can be easily attributed to it. But the outer ripples, the ultimate outcome of the stone being tossed into the pond, are much more remote, more difficult to measure, and more difficult to attribute to the effects of the stone. When developing outcome indicators and targets, authorities should identify all the layers of ripples for a service, then work in from the outermost ripples until a measurable target can be identified. The example shown here is simplified – most services will have many more ripples. But the technique is a good one for identifying the best outcome measures.

EXHIBIT 2

## The ripple effect

This exhibit shows how the ripple effect could be used to identify outcome measures for food safety work. Councils should work from the outermost ripples until a measurable target can be identified.

*Source: Audit Commission*

**40.** Wycombe District Council has introduced training for staff in developing outcome indicators in this way [CASE STUDY 5].

**41.** Targeting and measuring the outcomes of a service are especially important because they tell you whether the service is achieving its purpose, rather than just whether it is running efficiently. But, in practice, you need to know that you are doing the thing right as well as doing the right thing – both efficiency and effectiveness are important.

CASE STUDY 5

### Wycombe District Council: focusing on outcomes

Wycombe District Council has been developing performance review over a number of years, progressively establishing a framework of strategic aims and objectives that is devolved to departments and to individual staff targets and has linked the organisation from top to bottom. Wycombe's developmental approach has helped to take staff along with it, and has helped to get their acceptance of the value of performance review and target setting. The council has also carried out regular public satisfaction surveys, and has used these to adjust its targets and prioritise services.

Recently, the council has adopted an ambitious policy to be 'in the bottom quartile for costs, and the top quartile for performance' in terms of nationally comparable indicators. But it has also been concerned that the performance review system now needs to concentrate on outcome measures, rather than just output and efficiency measures. This approach supplements a well-established quality improvement programme.

Because the council also believes that performance measures should always be developed from service-level staff rather than imposed from the top of the organisation, it organised a series of seminars to help heads of service to develop outcome indicators and targets for their services, and to discuss them with each other.

Because performance review has been developed step by step over many years in Wycombe, the council has a well-established framework of aims, objectives and targets at all levels, with which staff are familiar. This has made it possible now to develop a more ambitious policy of service improvement, and a more comprehensive set of performance measures at all levels that better reflects the outcomes that the council wants to achieve.

## At what levels should targets be set?

**42.** Once a council, police force or fire brigade has decided which areas to prioritise for targets and standards, it then has to decide the levels at which to set its targets, or what levels of service to promise in its service standards. When doing this, authorities should:

- involve members, the public and staff;
- use information on past performance;
- use national standards and codes of practice where available; and
- consider the authority's corporate and departmental objectives.

**43.** Overall, targets should be set at a level that stretches the organisation, but which does not demoralise staff by being unrealistic. The new statutory framework proposed by the Government is a useful start when thinking about targets for national performance indicators, and some councils have already adopted this as an overall policy aim (see Case Study 5). But for locally developed targets, there may be no available data or comparisons. Getting the level right may be a matter of experience, based on previous targets and future plans. When organisations set targets for the first time they sometimes get them wrong because they do not have adequate information on past performance. Before setting a target, particularly one which is intended to achieve public accountability, it may be useful first to monitor the service to find out how it is performing at present, and what kind of improvement is possible.

*Targeting and measuring the outcomes of a service are especially important because they tell you whether the service is achieving its purpose.*

*A solution to this dilemma may be to adopt different 'layers' of targets.*

## How many targets should be set?

**44.** In deciding how many targets to set, and how many services should be subject to targets and standards, councils, police forces and fire brigades should bear in mind two conflicting principles. To adopt too few targets may mean that too much attention is paid to the services that are targeted at the expense of those that are not. On the other hand, too many targets may mean that authority members and senior officers cease to take them seriously, the importance of each one diluted because there are so many of them [**BOX F**]. A solution to this dilemma may be to adopt different 'layers' of targets, with the lowest layer set by front-line managers and reported only to front-line staff, higher layers set by and reported to senior officers and members, and a top layer of key corporate and major service targets reported to the public.

**45.** But even if this layered approach is used, authorities still have to decide how many targets to have in each 'layer'. And these decisions need careful management – members may feel excluded if they think targets and performance information are being withheld from them.

**BOX F**

**Too many targets**

'At one time, we seemed to have thousands of targets, and they were all reported to committee. Because there were so many, no-one took them seriously, especially members. They've been cut down a lot now though – I think that's helped to make people take notice of them.'

*– Performance review officer, district council*

## How can quality be measured?

**46.** Many councils, police forces and fire brigades, and the Audit Commission, have sought to develop indicators and targets for service 'quality'. The problem with measuring and targeting quality is that 'quality' is difficult to define. A 'good quality' benefits service, for example, may be one that ensures that benefit take-up is maximised and that advises claimants on the full range of benefits available. But it would not be 'good quality' if it took ten weeks to process each new claim, if assessments were inaccurate or if fraudulent claims were not detected: quality has many aspects and cannot be considered in isolation from efficiency.

**47.** Public satisfaction is often cited as a good proxy for quality. For many services this is true. Refuse collection, street cleaning, housing benefits, and housing repairs are all services where quality can be assessed in large measure through consumer satisfaction. But for some services, the perception of what is a 'quality' service may vary between different people. In libraries, for example, different people may want different kinds of books and facilities. Town planning is notoriously fraught with sharply conflicting local views on what is 'good' and what is 'bad'. And public demands for 'more bobbies on the beat' may be at odds with what is known to be the most effective way of preventing and detecting crime. The difficulty of using user satisfaction as a proxy for quality is particularly acute in social services, where service users' interests often conflict and satisfaction can be difficult to assess. When a child on the at-risk register is taken into care, for example, one desired outcome – protecting the child – may be achieved. But the child's parents are unlikely to be satisfied with the situation, and a child's satisfaction with the service is also much harder to ascertain than that of a tenant or library user.

**48.** There may also be 'global' issues to take into account, such as equality of opportunity and environmental sustainability. These affect all services, and should be targeted within any set of indicators. Milton Keynes Unitary Authority has recognised this multi-faceted approach to the idea of 'quality' [CASE STUDY 6, overleaf]. It can also be achieved by targeting public satisfaction not just for the whole population, but for the different communities and groups within it, ensuring that people with special interests and needs are getting as good a deal as the rest of the community.

*For some services, the perception of what is a 'quality' service may vary between different people.*

**49.** Quality, then, cannot usually be captured with a single target. It needs a balanced group of targets and performance measures to make sure that it is achieved. Whether the targets applied to a service adequately capture its quality is a good test for any service standard.

*Quality has many aspects and cannot be considered in isolation from efficiency.*

**CASE STUDY 6**

**Milton Keynes Unitary Authority: measuring quality and outcomes**

Milton Keynes' performance review system concentrates on targeting and measuring the quality and outcomes of services, but also makes it clear that quality can be assessed only by looking at a whole service and whether it is achieving its intended outcomes. There is also an emphasis on a corporate approach, where all parts of the council develop quality services consistently.

The council has begun to develop indicators and standards in areas where this has traditionally proved to be difficult, such as children's social services. This has also led to a new interdirectorate and interagency approach to standards and targets, with the learning and development directorate now thinking about targets for 'lifelong learning', developed in conjunction with other adult education providers. The council believes that breaking down barriers with other agencies is important, and has also started to develop community safety targets with the police.

Milton Keynes has taken the opportunity of its new unitary status to develop many new ideas about targets, performance review, and interagency working, and intends to consult the public throughout this development process. As one councillor put it: 'We need to keep up the public pressure on us, but we need to make sure we can deliver as a result of the pressure. We need to be sure that the council makes a real difference to people.'

## How can organisations set interagency targets?

**50.** Many of the issues of greatest concern to local communities cut across local authority departments, and across different service providers: community safety, community health, transport and environmental quality are good examples of these sorts of issues. This has been recognised by the Government, which has proposed a new role for councils in co-ordinating local interagency working, and a new duty to secure the economic, social and environmental well-being of the area (Refs. 1 and 2). Partnership working is looked at in more detail in the Audit Commission's management paper, *A Fruitful Partnership* (Ref. 5).

**51.** While many councils, police forces and fire brigades are working jointly with other public, private and voluntary sector bodies, few have set standards or targets in these areas. Setting interagency performance indicators is difficult.[1] In devising local indicators for youth crime, for example, district councils need to establish common ground with the police, the county council, the probation service, the magistrates' courts and the crown courts. These organisations operate over areas covered by different boundaries, set different targets, are subject to different statutory standards, and measure different things or the same things in different ways.

**52.** Some authorities, however, have begun to tackle these problems. Bradford Metropolitan Council has developed interagency indicators for community safety with the police and probation services **[CASE STUDY 7, overleaf]**.

*Setting interagency performance indicators is difficult ... Some authorities, however, have begun to tackle these problems.*

1 Local audits following the Commission's 1997 report on youth crime showed that 'most local authorities found data collection difficult' (Ref. 6).

CASE STUDY 7

## Bradford Metropolitan Council: interagency indicators and targets

Bradford has overcome some of the problems associated with developing these indicators by working closely with other organisations to develop compatible sets of data. So, for example, the police now collect detailed information on crime according to the postcode for the area in which the crime was committed. The council then collates this information using GIS (geographical information system) software, so that it can be recalculated within any chosen geographical boundary. This overcomes the problems associated with different organisations covering different geographical areas, and enables crime figures for the 'overlapping' areas covered by different agencies to be established.

Using not only hard data related to reported crime figures, but also perceptual data from surveys carried out through the council's citizens panel, the council, police and other agencies have developed outcome indicators that focus on both the fear of crime and actual crime.

### *Fear of crime*

These indicators include:

- an increase in the proportion of people who feel safe in Bradford;
- a decrease in the proportion of people who think they will be victims of crime;
- an increase in the proportion of people who feel safe in:
  - their homes;
  - their neighbourhoods; and
- a reduction in the proportion of people who have changed their behaviour as a result of fear of being victimised.

### *Actual crime*

These indicators include:

- number of offences committed by young people;
- number of young offenders;
- number of property crimes; and
- number of crimes against the person.

Targets for these indicators will be set to monitor the success of interagency community safety initiatives that are now being developed.

# 4. Measuring the achievement of targets

**53.** Setting unmonitored targets is likely to be counterproductive, because of the risk that organisations will assume that targets are being met, while local people experience something rather different. This scenario can be worse than having no targets at all. And if targets cannot be monitored, there is no way of reviewing them and therefore no information available on which to plan improvements. If you don't know whether you're meeting your target this year, how can you know what kind of target to set for next year?

**54.** The main obstacles to effective monitoring are staff resistance and the potential costs of collecting data. The next section looks at how these problems can be tackled, but begins by looking at why comprehensive performance review systems are important.

## Performance review systems: why they're so important

**55.** Local performance indicators have always been of limited value unless they are incorporated into a comprehensive review system.[I] Best value recognises this reality, and will require councils, police forces and fire brigades to develop their local indicators and targets as part of a wider process of fundamental performance review and local performance planning.

**56.** One of the two main functions of a performance review system is to improve the council's performance overall. The London Borough of Newham believes that its close attention to performance monitoring has helped it to move from 31st to within the top 12 in its own composite 'league table' of London boroughs within two years – by far the best improvement achieved by any London borough **[CASE STUDY 8, overleaf]**.

*If you don't know whether you're meeting your target this year, how can you know what kind of target to set for next year?*

I The Commission has published a number of national value-for-money studies that pursue this point; in particular, *Calling the Tune – Performance Management in Local Government* (Ref. 7).

CASE STUDY 8

## London Borough of Newham: improving performance overall

Performance information derived from a wide range of indicators is reported to a leader's panel every month. If performance is found to be deteriorating, members can (and frequently do) ask for reports to be submitted to the next panel on how performance is to be improved. This direct involvement of the council leadership ensures that the process is taken seriously, and action always results from the panel's decisions. It has enabled Newham, in the two years since the panel's inception, to move from 31st to within the top dozen in their locally derived London league table of performance, using a composite indicator compiled by the council from rankings within a selected group of national indicators.

Council officers believe that local performance indicators are a powerful tool in Newham because they are relevant to service delivery. Performance monitoring on a regular basis against a wide range of local indicators has become part of the staff's day-to-day routines; staff find the resulting up-to-date information helpful in running their services and can adjust services to tackle problems as soon as they arise. As the leader of the council put it:

'Local indicators must reflect processes where managers have control. If the indicators identify a problem, managers must know why this is happening.'

Using benchmarking data, initially in relation to London authorities, the council's aim is to be at the top of its comparative league table. This is a simple but powerful motivator for members and staff alike. However, it can be achieved only by continual reference to accurate and comparable performance measures. To achieve this kind of comparative measurement, the council has made sure that its computer systems can generate the information automatically wherever possible.

The council intends to achieve a 5 per cent reduction in costs and a 10 per cent increase in quality (judged using a basket of indicators including the national performance indicators) over a three-year period.

Newham's experience demonstrates that it is important for local performance indicators to have the support of the political leadership. The extent to which the performance and efficiency review process has embedded itself in the day-to-day management of the council has been due to the priority attached to it by the leader of the council.

**57.** Good performance review systems operate cyclically **[EXHIBIT 3]**, by:

- deriving departmental objectives from corporate aims and objectives;
- using targeted performance measures to assess how well objectives are being achieved;
- devolving responsibility for indicators and targets to individual staff;
- assessing the achievement of personal targets through performance appraisal mechanisms;
- aggregating this performance information and proposed future targets at a departmental level;
- reporting information to authority members and senior officers; and
- using the results to review objectives.

EXHIBIT 3

**The performance review cycle**

Local indicators should be part of a comprehensive performance review cycle.

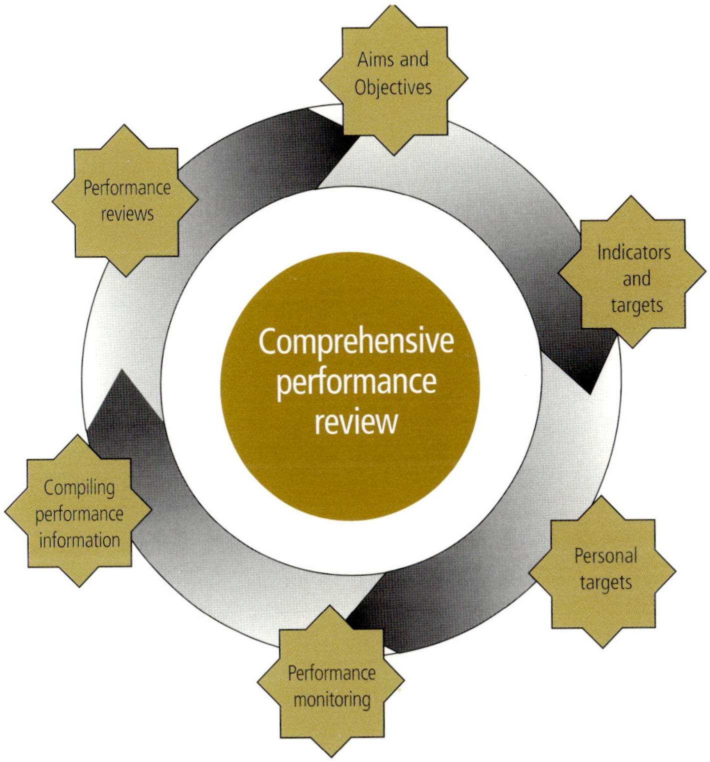


*Source: Audit Commission*

**58.** In recent years, some councils, police forces and fire brigades have begun to incorporate public consultation processes into their cyclical performance review systems, using feedback from the public to review targets and objectives. This approach, which takes the process of performance review a step forward, and provides a basis for achieving best value, has been adopted by South Somerset District Council [**CASE STUDY 9**]. The importance of public consultation and involvement in setting targets is discussed in detail later in this paper.

**59.** Where authorities have no performance review system in place, the task of setting one up on a corporate basis and in line with the best value framework may seem daunting, particularly for unitary councils or larger authorities. This is especially true where there is a strongly departmental culture with relatively independent service departments, or where a new unitary council has been formed from different district councils with quite different management cultures. North Lincolnshire Council, a relatively new unitary council, has grasped the nettle and decided to set up comprehensive performance review across the whole council from scratch [**CASE STUDY 10, overleaf**].

**60.** Without comprehensive performance review, targets, performance indicators, community consultation and even staff appraisal sit rather uncomfortably on the surface of the organisation, with no clear links to policy priorities and commitments. There is also a danger that performance information will not be used properly. Performance review systems help to build these processes into the organisation's core activities, and make sure that the resulting information is used effectively.

*Without comprehensive performance review, targets, performance indicators, community consultation and even staff appraisal sit rather uncomfortably on the surface of the organisation...*

## Staff resistance

**61.** Initial staff resistance to gathering performance data can be overcome if staff believe that the information is going to be useful to them as well as to others; that is, if they feel some ownership of the data. Getting staff to 'buy in' to the process is also one of the best ways of ensuring that data will be collected carefully and accurately. In one district council, for example, staff in the benefits and revenues section were initially resistant to producing performance information because they thought that it would be used to punish them for poor performance. But by closely involving staff in deciding what kind of information should be collected, this fear was overcome. Then, when monitoring took place and performance information became available to staff, they found it useful. And as the process of data collecting and reporting became incorporated into day-to-day activities, the burden turned out to be lighter than they had expected it to be.

CASE STUDY 9

### South Somerset District Council: connecting consultation and performance review

South Somerset has a comprehensive performance review system, with corporate objectives and targets linked to area and unit ones, which are in turn linked to individual targets through staff appraisal. The process is also linked to the council's extensive public consultation process, which follows a carefully planned annual cycle.

The council has a decentralised structure, with all decisions taken at four area committees. Most budgets are devolved to these area committees – the council believes this is a key to getting people involved. The council is not structured around traditional departments and committees; councillors, along with officers, take part instead in topic panels and groups that cover issues such as the environment, social welfare, or arts and recreation. These panels are open to the public, and are designed to discuss issues rather than to take decisions around fixed recommendations like traditional committees. Through these panels and the area committees, the council sets targets for a wide range of services, and monitors their achievement using local performance indicators. Some of the targets apply to the whole council, but some are different for the different decentralised areas.

To involve local people further, the council interviewed around 300 local people in 1998 to ask them detailed questions about how the budget should be spent – this information was used in setting budget priorities and service targets. The council also has a consultative panel of around 1,000 people. Because South Somerset is a rural area with mostly small communities, the council also organises 'village planning days' to consult people in the more remote communities. Town and parish councils are also involved in consultation processes – South Somerset has 121 of them. Involving these local councils in consultation has helped to make the parish councils more active and better attended.

South Somerset's localised, consultative approach was a councillor initiative, and has remained strongly councillor-led. Because councillors in South Somerset believe that they have achieved a real cultural change in the organisation, they have remained enthusiastically involved in sustaining and developing consultative processes, which they believe have strengthened their role and voice within the council machinery.

CASE STUDY 10

**North Lincolnshire Council: setting up a performance review system from scratch**

North Lincolnshire was created from two old districts and part of an abolished county. The new council had no clear organisational identity, and both members and officers felt that it was important to establish a clear 'North Lincolnshire culture' from the beginning. The council had inherited hundreds of performance indicators from the pre-existing councils, but felt that these provided little useful information. So the new council decided to discard all the existing performance indicators and set up an entirely new performance review system.

The new system was developed in consultation with service managers to make sure that the new targets and indicators would be of use to them, and to help them to see how the whole system fitted together and what their part in it would be. The council began by adopting a set of overall strategic aims and objectives, and devolved these down to 'service-level' and 'operational-level' objectives. Objectives, indicators and targets for 130 different services were summarised in single sheet service plans. At the heart of the North Lincolnshire system is a management workbook that explains not only how the overall system works, but also gives detailed guidance to managers on how to design good performance measures and how to set targets. So the managers themselves derive performance measures for their services, in line with these detailed guidelines. Targets, too, will be derived from the 'bottom up', with councillors eventually being asked to approve the targets that have been developed by staff.

Targets for all services will be shown against 'standard performance' levels that have been derived from comparative and benchmarking data from other councils, and other sectors where this is available.

The project is an ambitious one, and the council expects that the system will change and develop in future years - in particular, to involve the public more closely in the development of council services - but this 'big bang' approach has put North Lincolnshire well ahead of most other councils in developing the kinds of performance review and target-setting systems that will be needed under best value.

## Minimising the cost of data collection

**62.** It is easy to exaggerate the cost or the effort required to collect local performance data effectively. Authorities, such as Newham Council, which have comprehensive sets of local indicators and targets, report that they are neither particularly difficult nor expensive to maintain. Certain steps can help to make collecting performance data simple:

- integrating performance and other information collection systems;
- using information technology; and
- using sampling.

### Integrating systems

**63.** Data collection systems can be automated or integrated into the day-to-day tasks of staff with minimal, if any, additional work. Whenever councils, police forces or fire brigades consider purchasing or developing new software, they should consider how the software is going to help to collect the data needed to monitor the achievement of targets for the service. This is particularly important in services such as social services or the processing of offenders by the police, where the information is held only on personal casefiles, and where authorities might be concerned about confidentiality if staff need to look at casenotes to calculate performance data.

**64.** However, where targets cannot be monitored automatically, authorities will need manual systems that collect data in a simple and accurate way, and which make sure the data is collected consistently for each monitoring period. 'Time-and-motion' techniques or flowcharts can help officers to work out a step-by-step process whereby they can gather performance data without significant additional work.

### Using technology

**65.** Information technology can be used to make data collection cheaper and simpler even in areas where, traditionally, relatively few authorities have managed to set up effective information systems. Cornwall County Council's social services department has introduced computer monitoring of social services casework, an area where it has been difficult to monitor performance by conventional means **[CASE STUDY 11, overleaf]**.

*Authorities which have comprehensive sets of local indicators and targets, report that they are neither particularly difficult nor expensive to maintain.*

CASE STUDY 11

## Cornwall County Council: using IT

Monitoring social services referrals, assessments and care packages can be a difficult task for any authority. In Cornwall, there are six district councils as well as the county council. Monitoring community care is made even more difficult by the fact that it is a large rural county, sparsely populated and with no large urban centres, and each local social services office operates with a high degree of autonomy.

At the start of care in the community in 1993, Cornwall introduced a number of new posts called 'case co-ordinators'. Their task was to deal with all the straightforward care in the community work. These staff use a care management system that is run on laptop computers to help them to manage cases by generating orders, authorisations for care packages and personalised care plans for clients. Care managers can use this system to ensure that work is progressing and to identify promptly changes to individual circumstances that might require plans to be changed.

At the start of care in the community, the council agreed timescales for all care management work with the local health authority. The extent to which these target timescales are met is monitored at both local and county-wide levels. The co-ordinators enter information on to the computerised care management system as they carry out their work and key data automatically generate messages to care managers to identify work that needs to be done or that has been carried out. In addition, key data can generate management reports to enable managers to monitor workloads and financial performance.

The council has found that the computers have been very popular with staff because they enable care packages to be organised and delivered more efficiently. Because management information about targets is a by-product of this operational system rather than the reason for it, staff see that monitoring information actually reflects their practice. Monitoring workloads and targets has become more acceptable as a result in a service that has traditionally been resistant to oversight.

Key targets are communicated to carers and social services clients through specific leaflets, so that they know what service to expect from the council. Around two-thirds of community care services are provided by the independent sector. Where services are provided by other organisations, targets are devolved to them and responsibility for monitoring against them is part of the council's contract agreement with the service provider.

**66.** Performance data needs to be held electronically on a computer spreadsheet or database which can be used to analyse the data and extract information on trends and comparisons. In some cases, there may be good off-the-peg software systems available for monitoring specific services (housing benefits and environmental health, for example). But, even where they are not, complicated bespoke database systems are not usually necessary. Commercially available off-the-shelf spreadsheet and database packages are powerful enough to undertake all the analysis and presentation of data that authorities are likely to need, and to allow comparative data from other sources - such as other authorities in a benchmarking group, or national databases such as the Audit Commission performance indicators or CIPFA data - to be added in.

## Sampling

**67.** Sampling can be an appropriate way to collect performance data, particularly if the number of 'events' in a statistical population is very large, and data cannot be collected automatically. Sampling also allows authorities to gain reliable information about aspects of performance, such as the accuracy with which benefit claims are assessed, that would otherwise be expensive or complicated to monitor comprehensively. The Commission has published a short paper giving good practice guidance on sampling.[1]

1 *Sampling guidance for performance indicators* is available from the Commission performance indicators helpline on 0171 828 1212.

# 5. Involving staff, authority members and the public

## Involving staff

**68.** Whether a service is provided directly by the authority or by a contractor or voluntary sector provider, it is essential that staff are involved in setting targets if they are to be committed to achieving them, and if councils, police forces and fire brigades are to use the knowledge that staff have about ways to improve services. This may seem obvious, but relatively few authorities currently involve staff in identifying what levels targets should be set at, or what aspects of services should be targeted, in anything other than a rather informal way.

**69.** Some authorities use staff appraisal systems to devolve corporate and departmental targets to individual staff. This helps to make staff feel that they are contributing to overall policy priorities and objectives. It helps them to see where they fit in. It also helps to make sure that all performance targets are attributed to named individuals. But where authorities devolve responsibility in this way, it is especially important that targets are realistic and that staff believe that they can achieve them. Assessing an individual's performance against a target that they believe to be unachievable is likely to be demotivating. Managers have a key role to play, however, in encouraging staff to be ambitious and aim for high levels of performance.

**70.** No matter how carefully staff are involved in identifying service targets, they should not actually prescribe them. Targets should be set only after a wider audience has been consulted, including service users. But, ultimately, it is the responsibility of members of councils and police or fire authorities to decide exactly what a target should be. This means that no matter how thorough the staff consultation, staff may still be required to hit targets that they believe are too ambitious. In the end, getting staff to buy in to targets which they initially believe are too ambitious is dependent largely on the skills of managers. But it will also depend on the culture of the organisation. Where an authority is already committed to continuous improvement, and has persuaded its staff that such a strategy makes sense, it will be easier to persuade staff to buy in to tough targets.

## Involving members

**71.** Where authority members are fully involved in setting targets and monitoring performance, corporate performance review systems and the process of setting and achieving targets are more likely to be sustained and to survive in the longer term. Most of the comprehensive performance review systems that have survived and flourished have been strongly member-led [**BOX G**]. The performance review systems in Redditch and South Somerset councils are good examples [**CASE STUDIES 12 overleaf, and 9**]. If members are involved, and are seen to be involved, the quality and accuracy of the data produced is likely to be higher, and staff throughout the organisation are likely to take the targets that have been set more seriously.

*No matter how carefully staff are involved in identifying service targets, they should not actually prescribe them.*

**BOX G**

**Member commitment**

'Setting up any kind of corporate system is notoriously difficult in a big county council like Kent. But members here are very keen to make sure their policy priorities are carried out, and they want to see exactly how each department is going to contribute to this. I think this strong member commitment has helped.'

– *Councillor, Kent County Council*

'The emphasis placed on performance monitoring here by members, and in particular by the leader, has helped to persuade officers to take it seriously. The close scrutiny given to the monthly performance reports by the leader's panel means that officers make absolutely sure the information is complete and accurate. They don't want to get caught out giving information which might later prove to have been misleading or even wrong.'

– *Policy officer, Newham Council*

*Getting staff to buy in to targets which they initially believe are too ambitious is dependent largely on the skills of managers.*

CASE STUDY 12

**Redditch Borough Council: performance review sustained by members**

Redditch Borough Council was one of the first councils to introduce a performance review system and in 1991 introduced a comprehensive set of local performance indicators and targets through a councillor-led initiative. For the first four years, the system was co-ordinated and run from the corporate centre. During this time, service departments gradually began to learn how to devise good performance indicators, and to appreciate their benefits. So the responsibility for devising indicators and compiling monitoring information was devolved away from the centre to heads of service.

The drive to establish performance monitoring in Redditch was strongly councillor-led, with councillors still taking a keen interest in the biannual monitoring reports to service committees. Some councillors have developed a special interest in particular services and groups of indicators, which has helped the process to continue and develop.

Over the last two years, the system has been developed further by involving the public more in planning and targeting council services. This is done primarily through 'neighbourhood groups' - quarterly open agenda meetings in each of the 14 town neighbourhoods. These meetings are chaired by a councillor. Since 1994 the council has also run the 'Redditch reports' initiative – one of the first of its kind in local government. A panel of 1,000 local residents is surveyed every six months through a detailed questionnaire on their opinions of the full range of council services.

The council also sends a community plan to every household each year, detailing the council's corporate objectives and targets. This has a tear-off slip for local people to comment on the council's proposals – 500 replies are received each year. Again, development and content of the community plan are strongly councillor-led.

Councillors in Redditch make sure that the comments received through all the consultation processes are taken into account in the way that the council prioritises and plans services. They believe that through consultation of this kind, particularly through 'Redditch reports', public satisfaction on services can be used by officers and members to set appropriate targets, rather than consulting people on exactly what those targets should be.

**CASE STUDY 13**

**Kent County Council: corporate targets driven by councillors**

Kent's key targets come directly from the council's strategic statement, following the 1997 elections, when political control of the council changed. This statement was very specific, covering a wide range of services with clear numerical targets. Some of these targets are ambitious and not directly within the council's control – for example, reducing sulphur dioxide emissions by 3 per cent, and increasing economic growth in the county to 3.3 per cent.

These targets have been used to develop a 'top-down, bottom-up' approach to performance monitoring, getting service departments to develop their own objectives and targets in their business plans which help the council to achieve its overall aims and targets as expressed in its strategic statement. The council's 60-odd service units have to develop both short- and long-term targets, including targets for service outcomes. Councillors have also been strongly involved in reviewing - and in some cases changing - these. In particular, members have rejected targets that are not measurable – emphasis has been placed on developing targets where it will be clear whether or not the council has achieved them.

The council's aims were drawn from consultation, including a county-wide 'Future Kent' survey which included wide-ranging interest group meetings. The council has communicated its key targets and aims to households in Kent through a newsletter. This has generated a lot of interest and feedback, probably because of the very specific promises that it makes. The council will follow this up with a wide range of consultative processes.

Kent's approach has been strongly member-driven, which has helped to pull together the different approaches that had previously existed in different services – this task is often difficult, especially in a big county council. But this difficulty has been balanced by allowing the unit managers themselves to come up with their own proposals for objectives and targets and by encouraging staff involvement.

**72.** If performance review is led by members, it is also more likely that targets will be relevant to the overall policy objectives and priorities of the council [**CASE STUDY 13**]. Where members nod through performance monitoring reports at committee meetings without discussion, unmet targets can simply pass by unnoticed. But where members give such reports proper scrutiny and demand explanations if targets have not been met, the chances of action being taken to improve poor performance are much higher. This is especially true where members were involved in setting the targets in the first place.

**73.** Previous Commission reports have highlighted the small proportion of members' time which is typically spent reviewing performance in many authorities (Ref. 8). In some authorities, members have found it difficult to see how performance monitoring can help them to play their roles effectively. This can be a missed opportunity for members, as performance indicators are a good way for them to hold staff and contractors to account for the way in which they have implemented members' policy priorities. Officers can encourage members to get involved by showing them how monitoring locally chosen indicators can make it easier for them to see whether their policies are being implemented effectively. Training can be useful here. An alternative approach is to get authority members involved through their interest in down-to-earth, front-line issues. By working with members with a particular interest in a particular service, staff in some authorities have been able to generate more of an interest in specific indicators and targets, and to develop new ones that address the issues that particular members consider to be important. New political structures of the kind proposed by the Government (Refs. 1 and 2) may also help to get members more involved.

**74.** If members are to play an effective role in setting and monitoring targets, they will need appropriate support and information. There is unlikely to be much benefit from members setting targets if they simply accept their officers' recommendations because they have no other information on which to base a judgement about what is achievable, for example. It is equally important for members to recognise that sometimes what is desirable may not be possible within available resources, or that a small improvement in performance may require a significant increase in resources. Simply demanding that an individual standard is achieved without considering the practical consequences, such as the knock-on effect on other services, is likely to demoralise staff and distort performance.

*Performance indicators are a good way for members to hold staff and contractors to account for the way in which they have implemented members' policy priorities.*

## Informing and involving the public

### Letting the public know about performance

**75.** About three-quarters of councils and police forces make some attempt to inform local people about the targets that they have set, and how they have performed against them, although some have done no more than publish the Audit Commission performance indicators. Under best value, all councils, police forces and fire brigades will need to publish local performance indicators as part of their local performance plans.

**76.** Published service standards aimed directly at service users are a good way of making clear what levels of service people can expect, and how the authority has performed in the past. York City Council has a set of 'customer contracts' presented in an attractive and eye-catching way for a wide range of services. These contracts make promises about the kind of service that users can expect to receive, as well as details of how the service works and what it can and cannot do **[BOX H]**.

**77.** Another way to get performance information and service standards across to people is through annual reports or other publications that are distributed to all households. To make such publications more useful and more likely to be kept, some councils combine them with an 'A-Z' directory of council services and contact numbers, or include contact numbers for ward councillors.

**BOX H**

**York City Council's Homelessness Charter**

**78.** Although getting information to everyone is important, some of the more obvious methods of distributing this kind of information may not be the most cost-effective. For example, research carried out by Brent Council found that information included with council tax bills is rarely read – so although more expensive, it may be more cost-effective to distribute information on standards and targets independently from existing mailings – particularly those asking for money.

**79.** The internet is an increasingly important route for disseminating information on service standards, targets and performance. While a relatively small proportion of the population currently has access to the internet, the number of households with internet connections is increasing every month, and existing public sector websites are well-used – Buckinghamshire County Council website received over 13,000 visits between August 1997 and August 1998. Internet sites also have the advantage of giving site visitors an opportunity for instant feedback. With internet access increasing rapidly, councils, police forces and fire brigades should use this relatively cheap opportunity to communicate with the public, and get feedback on what they think about the authority's performance.

## Involving the public in setting standards and targets

**80.** There are three identifiable steps to involving the public fully in setting local standards and targets:

- communication – telling the public what your targets are and whether you have met them;
- consultation – telling the public what your targets are and whether you have met them, and asking whether they think this is satisfactory; and
- involvement – asking the public what they think your targets should be and what levels they should be set at [BOX I].

**BOX I**

**Consultation and involvement**

'When you consult people, you put things on the agenda. When you involve them, they make up their own agenda. That's the difference.'

– *National Consumer Council officer*

*Under best value, all councils, police forces and fire brigades will need to publish local performance indicators as part of their local performance plans.*

**81.** Our research shows that most authorities are at the first stage, with about one-quarter edging into the second. Few have reached the third stage. Consulting and involving the public in setting local standards will be an essential element of best value, so authorities will need to develop good practice in this area quickly.

**82.** Finding out what standards the public would like to see set can be integrated with other forms of consultation or feedback. Many authorities conduct surveys of local residents and these can help to set targets for the future. Councils, police forces and fire brigades which are intending to set up new community consultation processes, or new performance review systems to meet best value requirements, should make sure that these processes are integrated and that consultation results can be used to plan and prioritise services, and to set appropriate targets.

**83.** A growing number of authorities use panel surveys as a cost-effective way of carrying out consumer research rather than random surveys. The results of panel surveys can be readily translated into performance targets, with targets set to improve overall levels of satisfaction with particular services. This is a good way of setting targets for service outcomes – public satisfaction with services is an outcome that any authority would always want to achieve, although it is not the only factor to consider (see paragraphs 45-48). Town, parish and community councils can also be a useful way to consult local communities, particularly where these are well-attended by local people. South Somerset Council has used parishes in this way **[CASE STUDY 9, p37]**. Focus groups and neighbourhood forums can also be used to influence targets and the way that services are planned.

**84.** One of the biggest obstacles to involving people in setting local standards is their perceived lack of interest in local government. Some authorities have found that attempts to recruit local panels have failed because no one was interested in joining. Others have found that local consultative forums get few attendees – and those who do attend are there only because they have a personal axe to grind. The message from those authorities which have been more successful seems to be: persevere. And if someone has an axe to grind, let them put their axe on the agenda. In South Somerset, community consultation meetings begin with an 'open' agenda, where attendees can get items of particular concern to them discussed before the main business of the meeting begins.

*People may not be particularly interested in educational achievement targets for a whole county, but they may well be interested in the performance of their local school.*

**85.** Another way of generating interest in local performance targets is to set them at levels which are of immediate local interest and relevance. People may not be particularly interested in educational achievement targets for a whole county, but they may well be interested in the performance of their local school, for example.

**86.** Few authorities consult the public directly on what specific individual targets should be. This may be partly because setting realistic targets involves balancing consumer demands with what the council can achieve, taking into account available resources and the competing priorities of different services. Some authorities have asked local people what they think targets should be – for example, 'do you think our target for processing planning applications within eight weeks should be 80 per cent or 90 per cent?'; or, 'do you think our targets for clearing up violent crimes should be 90 per cent or 95 per cent?' But to make an informed decision, people need a lot of information about current performance, any costs associated with raising the target and how the priorities given to different services might have to be balanced – otherwise they will simply opt for the higher number.

**87.** Despite these difficulties, there are some examples of local people taking the initiative in setting targets and standards for the services that they receive in their own community. An example of this is the work done by the National Consumer Council (NCC) with tenants on a council housing estate in the West Midlands **[CASE STUDY 14]**. And those authorities where community consultation has become well-established are beginning to consider ways to involve people more fully, to ask them what targets they think the council should be setting, rather than asking them if the council's targets are right.

CASE STUDY 14

### National Consumer Council: a pilot study on community involvement

The NCC has carried out six pilot projects to help local people to get involved in developing their own public service charters. One of these pilots involved working with a group of tenants in a West Midlands housing estate of around 2,000 tenants.

Initially, the NCC worked with the tenants' association to devise a questionnaire survey for a sample of the estate's tenants. The survey asked people what they thought was most important in providing a good quality housing service. The survey was carried out using door-to-door interviews, some of which were conducted by tenants' association members. The survey asked open questions about 'the most important issues', as well as giving tenants lists of factors to prioritise.

The results of the survey were discussed with tenants at an 'open day' at a local school. Attendance was encouraged by holding a prize draw and organising face painting and badge making activities for children. From this discussion and analysis of the survey results, a draft estate charter was drawn up.

The council already had standards and targets for some of the priorities in the draft charter. Most of the tenants had never heard of them. Through a process of negotiation with council officers, targets were developed for the charter that took account of what the tenants wanted, and what the council felt it was able to deliver. Two dozen key standards emerged.

Further meetings were held with staff and the tenants' association members to finalise the charter. Eventually, the tenants took the finished charter along to a meeting with the council's chair and director of housing, and persuaded them to adopt it as council policy for the estate.

An action plan was then drawn up by a staff/tenant working group which set out who was responsible for each standard and how tenants would be involved in monitoring performance and revising the charter. Involving tenants in the details of implementation has produced many insights into how the service can be improved.

Although resource-intensive, this approach provides a good model for community involvement in setting local standards.

## Community consultation and charters – do they go together?

**88.** Some councils have developed their own overall 'citizen's charters', while others have developed separate charters for different services, which give detailed commitments about what kind of service users are entitled to, and how service users should be treated. Advice on how to draw up such charters is detailed in the Cabinet Office publication, *Service First: The New Charter Programme* (Ref. 9).

**89** Three or four years ago, many councils were writing these charter-style standards for their services. Since then, some of the councils that were in the forefront of this movement have now abandoned their charters. There seem to be three main reasons for this:

- a perception that charters have become discredited and may be counterproductive if people do not believe in them **[CASE STUDY 15]**;
- a tendency for charters to be inflexible (depending largely on 'all-the-time' targets which cannot easily be adjusted in the light of changing public expectations) and to get out of date quickly; and
- charters may not fit well with community consultation processes, giving the impression that services are 'handed down' by the council rather than planned with the community.

CASE STUDY 15

### London Borough of Brent local survey on charters

The London Borough of Brent was one of the first councils to adopt service charters, publishing a comprehensive set of charters and making them available through council offices. In 1995, the council undertook research into how successful these charters had been in raising public awareness of the kinds of services and service standards that they could expect from the council.

The survey revealed that around a half of local residents knew nothing at all about any of the charter standards – this figure was much the same for specific service users. And another third said that they knew 'just a little'. Only three in ten people who had visited council offices recalled even seeing the charter leaflets. Only 41 per cent of respondents thought that charters in general were useful, and only one-third thought that charters helped to raise the standards of service that people receive.

However, more detailed qualitative research showed that people did want comprehensible information on council services, and that it should be displayed more widely. The problem seemed to arise with the idea of a 'charter' that made promises without asking people what they wanted. Overall, the research revealed that there was a demand for accessible information which addressed people's needs, rather than 'promises' that the public did not expect would be kept.

*Making clear what kind of service has been established after consultation is important.*

**90.** These points are valid ones, and are addressed in the relaunched Cabinet Office guidance on charters. The National Consumer Council project **[CASE STUDY 14, p51]** demonstrates that a charter that reflects users' views or is created by them is possible, but may require a high level of resources.

**91.** However, there is a danger that if authorities abandon published charter standards for their services, they will not replace them with anything more useful to local people. Even quite intensive and regular consultation on services may leave local people unclear about what kinds of services they can expect and what targets have been agreed. Making clear what kind of service has been established after consultation is important, even if some of the glossy charters that authorities had begun to develop were simply too expensive to update regularly.

# 6. The cutting edge: where next?

**92.** The National Consumer Council project demonstrates that it is possible to get the public involved in setting local standards and targets where they believe it is of direct relevance to them, and where they believe that their involvement will improve the services that they are receiving. But there are significant barriers that authorities need to overcome. Big efforts will be needed to get local communities sufficiently involved – but once they are, the evidence from pilot studies suggests that communities themselves will then put in the effort, and will begin to set the agenda for what kinds of services they want and what kinds of targets should be set.

**93.** Other initiatives currently in use by local authorities may also provide a key for future community involvement in setting local standards and targets. The 'Planning for Real' system **[BOX J]** used by some councils could be adapted to consult local communities not just on planning issues, but on standards and targets in areas such as streetlighting, highway repairs, beat policing, housing repairs, and other 'street-level' issues, moving on to issues like educational achievement which have a local focus. The approach could be particularly useful if extended to interagency working, looking at issues such as community safety by using neighbourhood models to examine performance against interagency targets for specific areas.

**94.** Taking community involvement a step further, councils, police forces and fire brigades could begin to set targets for issues that are outside their direct remit, and which need the co-operation of the local community to achieve. Kent County Council has gone some way towards this with its target to improve air quality **[CASE STUDY 13, p47]**. But possibly the best example of this kind of initiative is provided by the Oregon state government in the USA, where a wide range of community outcome targets have been set, with the express purpose of getting local people involved in achieving goals over which the state has limited influence **[CASE STUDY 16, overleaf]**. This approach fits closely with the ideas expressed in recent white papers (Refs. 1 and 2), which proposed a new statutory duty for councils to promote the economic, social and environmental well-being of their area.

**BOX J**

**Neighbourhood Initiatives Foundation: 'Planning for Real'**

The Neighbourhood Initiatives Foundation is a national charity specialising in community participation. 'Planning for Real'[1] was developed in the 1970s as a tool to overcome communication barriers in housing estates where the normal channels had broken down. The method has evolved and can be applied to anything from a small patch of land to strategic planning. It has been used successfully in Britain, Europe, Africa and the United States.

Using a three-dimensional kit, local people make a big model of their own neighbourhood on a scale large enough to identify their own front door. Over 300 option cards are provided (including blank ones), so that people can arrange and rearrange the cards on the model to show what is needed and explore different ways of getting what is wanted. By focusing on the model, the method allows for a practical means of non-confrontational communication because once an option card is laid on the model it becomes anonymous. The experience of the Foundation is that sections of the community not previously involved in consultation will put their ideas forward.

The process gives the local community a 'voice', and the professional a clear idea of local people's needs. One council officer with experience of this approach commented: 'People involved in Planning for Real have said how much they enjoyed it and how much more real it became to them actually having a model rather than plans ... people cannot visualise plans.'

1 'Planning for Real' is a registered trademark. Organisations wishing to run exercises described as 'Planning for Real' events should first contact the Foundation to discuss using the technique to its full effect and to obtain permission for the use of the trademark (telephone 01952 590777).

*Source: Audit Commission research*

*It is possible to get the public involved in setting local standards and targets where they believe it is of direct relevance to them, and where they believe that their involvement will improve the services that they are receiving.*

CASE STUDY 16

**Oregon Shines: setting ambitious quality of life outcome targets**

In 1996, the Oregon state government adopted a strategic plan called 'Oregon Shines II'. The plan has three strategic goals for the state. These are:

- safe, caring and engaged communities;
- quality jobs for all Oregonians; and
- healthy, sustainable surroundings.

Attached to these overall goals are more specific objectives that go well beyond what state governments would normally be expected to influence. These include:

- Oregon's workforce will be the best educated and trained in America by the year 2000, and equal to any in the world by 2010;
- Oregon's per capita income will reach the national average by 2000, and be 10 per cent above the national average by 2010; and
- more Oregonians will be healthy and self-sufficient.

Achievement of these and other objectives is measured by a detailed set of performance indicators and key outcome measures. These outcome measures cover a wide range of social and economic outcomes, including child abuse, adult literacy, air and water pollution levels, women and ethnic minorities in senior company positions, educational achievement, poverty, and even participation by Oregon citizens in voluntary work.

The system depends on general support from the people of Oregon for the overall aims of 'Oregon Shines', and the state government acknowledges that the objectives and goals can be achieved only with the co-operation of its citizens. So all Oregonians have been provided with a list of actions that they can take to help to achieve the 'Oregon Shines' goals. Most of these are quite specific, and include getting to know your neighbours, reading to a school age child, preparing a résumé for someone looking for work, participating in local community groups and school governing bodies, planting trees, taking the bus to work, car-sharing, and organising recycling activities.

American state governments do have much greater powers to influence people's behaviour than do British local authorities – for example, through state taxes. Nevertheless, the programme is ambitious, considering the lack of trust that the American public has had in recent years in both federal and state governments. It remains to be seen whether 'Oregon Shines II' is as successful as its predecessor plan.

*Source: Oregon Shines 2, Oregon Progress Board, 1996. From Oregon state government website: http://www.econ.state.or.us*

**95.** Moving forward to full community involvement will mean councils working with their communities, with other service providers such as the NHS and schools, and with local businesses, to establish targets and service standards for broad issues that affect the community, rather than just for those services that they directly provide. The steps made by some authorities over the last few years towards engaging and involving communities make them well-placed to take up these new challenges, and the new Government has proposed both duties and powers to support community planning.

**96.** Although it is important that councils develop local standards and targets covering the quality of life in communities, they should not neglect the task of setting standards for the economy, efficiency and effectiveness of their own services as a result. These two strands of work should be seen as complementary and mutually reinforcing, not as alternatives to one another.

*Although it is important that councils develop local standards and targets covering the quality of life in communities, they should not neglect the task of setting standards for the economy, efficiency and effectiveness of their own services.*

# 7. Conclusion

**97.** While a significant number of councils, police forces and fire brigades are setting targets and monitoring performance in at least some of their services, most have a long way to go if they are to meet the challenge of best value effectively. And most of the authorities that do set targets and monitor performance against them still need to learn from the best authorities if they are to involve the public fully in the way that they plan and target services. Moreover, there are some areas where almost all authorities have a great deal to do to meet their obligations under new government initiatives – developing interagency targets for community safety, for example.

**98.** Best value and other legislation such as the Crime and Disorder Act will force the pace. Councils, police forces and fire brigades that have not already done so need to start setting up proper performance review systems, monitoring performance against targets and involving the public in setting and reviewing targets. Authorities should start work now, to make sure that their systems are running effectively by the time best value becomes a statutory requirement. Without clear, challenging local standards and targets, embracing all the ideas outlined in this paper, councils, police forces and fire brigades will find it difficult to demonstrate that they are achieving best value.